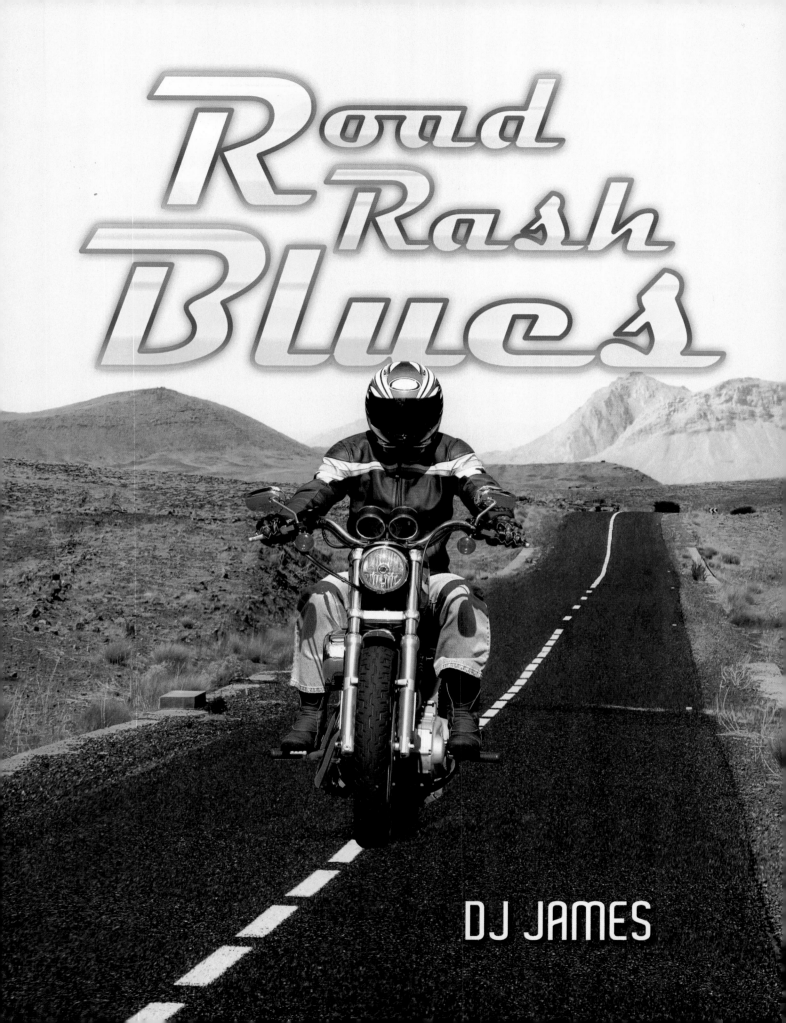

AuthorHouse™ UK
1663 Liberty Drive
Bloomington, IN 47403 USA
www.authorhouse.co.uk
UK TFN: 0800 0148641 (Toll Free inside the UK)
UK Local: 02036 956322 (+44 20 3695 6322 from outside the UK)

Because of the dynamic nature of the Internet, any web addresses or links contained in this book may have changed
since publication and may no longer be valid. The views expressed in this work are solely those of the author and do
not necessarily reflect the views of the publisher, and the publisher hereby disclaims any responsibility for them.

Any people depicted in stock imagery provided by Getty Images are models,
and such images are being used for illustrative purposes only.
Certain stock imagery © Getty Images.

This book is printed on acid-free paper.

ISBN: 978-1-6655-8368-8 (sc)
ISBN: 978-1-6655-8369-5 (e)

Print information available on the last page.

Published by AuthorHouse 01/08/2021

authorHOUSE®

The Best things in life are......

The emotions there are no words for,

And biker chicks that make you feel them.

Animal

This book is for the Brothers I've met, and have yet to meet.

For old ladies past, present, & future.

Bike Free.

Animal
N.M.C.

But most of all for <u>Denise</u> a Brother's

Ol Lady who Revved me up each time I stalled.

I love ya

<u>Animal</u>

Harley Heaven

A kick or two, or three or four,
    a curse, a kick, a booming roar,
The rider mounts, he knows the score.
And through the streets they move so loud,
A bike, a man — a brother who's proud.
The hassles gone, his heart is filled
With life and hope all fears are stilled.
Though rain may pour and snow may fall,
Never silenced is that call.
To freedom and a life so good,
Filled with feelin's of brotherhood.
Riding on both fast & slow,
There's always one more place to go,
where parties are and brothers gather
And laugh to think there's some who'd rather
call them down, then hide in shame
Wishing only to be the same, as these,
there men of strength and steel
Who ride to live, and live to feel
That wind in face's, hair and eye's,
Instead of letting time slip by.
So when you see us rumbling through,
Look hard and long co's we're the few
who know our minds, and feel our souls
And chore our life & worthy goals.
Ride on, ride free, and live your way.
In Harley Heaven we'll meet someday.

Animal (N.M.C.)

My Motor

The wind & the wild, they call for me,
The long open road that sets me free.
My wheels are turning toward newer way's
Highways of Heaven have filled my day's.

People in a panic, they rush here & there,
People who worry, they just stop and stare.
I'd like to share my freedom & emotion,
But I just keep my chopper in motion.

The machine that I ride is shiny & black,
She's a Tribra-chop as a matter of fact.
I keep her strong, she's my one and only,
As long as I'm on her, I'll never be lonely.

Animal (N.M.C.)

Road Rash Blues

If your a Biker, wrong or right.
Its gonna catch you late one night,
Outlaw or Angel you pay your due's
To the evil menace, The Road Rash Blues.

The 'Asphalt Reaper' will bide his time
And wait till your do'in about ninety—nine,
Then when you feel your startin to cruise
You'll find your doing the Road Rash Blues.

I'm not the kind of dude to ride in cars
I take my bike when I prop up bars,
Thats why I'm trying there scars to lose
All brought on by the Road Rash Blues.

Now every person born gotta die someday
And I'll die on my bike if I have my way.
But till my time comes I'll pay my due's
And keep on do'in the Road Rash Blues.

Animal (N.M.C.)

Missing You

Empty hearted, empty bed,

Words are written, left unsaid.

Care will perish miles apart,

Wish my Triumph would bloody start.

Animal (N.M.C.)

Bad News

My bike won't start,
I'm out of beer,
I can't depart,
My bike won't start.
It break's my heart
To just sit here,
My bike won't start,
I'm out of beer!

(April/May 80)
Animal (N.M.C.)

Ol' Lady

She's a dirty ol' lady that some call obscene,

But she's okay with me in her dirty old jeans

In her dirty old leathers, on my dirty old bike,

I'm her dirty ol' man, cause thats what I like.

Animal (N.M.C.)
(Liz Summer/Winter 79)

Remember

(To Anne with thanks)

Feelin, wheelin, jamming free
Chrome on steel blastin past,
Staccato engines roar & thunder
how riders high on Californian grass.
Ripping up fresh virgin road
Headlights crash against the night,
Shocking square john's in there beds
Squealing kids awake in fright.
Hells dark chariots vibrating free
Exhaust sparks crack in fiery glee,
Fumes & vapours from hogs on high
Then I awake, and the memories die.
The bars are still here, & the walls of cream
But where are you, was it just a dream,
Can we still climb those mountains high
And watch the castles as they float by.
Leave behind the dirty town
Find a small cottage & settle down,
Where mountain streams can bubble & foam
And birds & animals are free to roam.
No more the smell of burning oil
The tyres scream & faulty coil,
The thrill of speed on the open road
The wind in my hair as the miles unfold.
All this is part and now has gone
But you and I, we still go on,
The thick gray walls won't stop us now
We'll ride again, someday, somehow.

Animal
(Summer 78)

Little Starr

(For Pam)

A little bit of baby, a little bit of whore.

Give some credit to the streets for they have raised one more.

A little bit of loneliness. To stop it – that depends

On the quantity of whisky & the quality of friends.

A little bit of slowing down is always out of range,

Out of right, out of mind. She never wants to change.

A little bit of happiness by living in the wind,

Satisfied with parties, with bikes, and with men.

A little bit of innocence, although its hard to see.

A little bit of wondering who the hell she's gonna be.

So I stayed with her a little bit and watched her cop a buzz.

And told her all the stories about the little bit I was.

Then I took her for a little while, & held her pretty tight.

I promised to my Little Starr she's going to be alright.

Animal
(Summer 79)

11

Fuck You

They used to tell me to grow up,

To get my ass in gear.

They used to say theres more to life

Than bikes and sex and beer.

They used to tell me all that stuff

When I was just a child.

They used to say I would regret

My living hard and wild.

I didn't pay attention then,

And that was long ago.

I wish that I could find a way

To let them plainly know

I didn't change my crazy ways,

And I don't plan to quit.

For what its worth, the advice they gave

Was simply full of shit.

Animal

Yeah

Snorting life and running love,

Living hard fits like a glove.

Smiles and parties, moving fast,

Its easy to forget the past.

With shiny bikes & crazy chicks

Living free in the land of kicks.

Animal

Double Barrelled

Attention, nympho biker chicks,

For you this dildos suited.

Lubricate with fifty-weight,

Batteries not included.

You'll love the soothing relief

You'll get from double vee.

Electric start is optional

Try one — get me free.

Animal

14

Pervert!

I want to suck your eyelids.

I want to pop your zits.

I want to lick your nostrils.

And ream out your armpits.

I want you to wear leather panties

And tie you to the bed.

And rip out your kidneys,

Through holes I've drilled in your head.

See, I don't really care

If your tits are rather dinky.

When we get done with foreplay,

We'll get down to being kinky.

Animal

To Fuckheads In Power

Two wheels and a motor is what we live for,

Some have bread but most are poor.

We live on booze, or smoke a few joints

But whatever you do, remember these points.

Its the wide open road and the wind in our face,

Smoke dope by the bail, drink beer by the case.

We follow no rules but those of the free,

We mind our own buissiness but you won't let us be

So go suck cock you white collared pigs,

And stuff all your flashy big Rolls-Royce rigs

Stick your heads up your ass'es and breath deep fools

C'os we don't need all your dictatorship rules.

We're the last of the cowboys and love open space,

So find something else to gripe about & get off our case.

Animal

16

Stoned (again)

He speaks the language of sex.

And she responds like the throttle,

Wide open.

Sweet cream, her skin,

Out of it, within

The boundaries of unadulterated passion.

And her position

Is secure.

For he has taught her

How to share.

And so it is.

The three of them,

Riding each other.

(Kim. Early 78)
Animal

Need

Sometimes I need you naked,

Sometimes I need you wild.

I need you to carry my embryo.

I need you to care for my child.

But most of all I need you,

This feeling I cannot deny.

For in my heart I need you

This love can never die.

(For Kate 76/77)
Animal

The Ending

Its alright, I'm only dying now,

My broken bones are really screaming now,

You hear my voice its hoars & rasping.

For every breath I'm really gasping.

My lifes blood mixes with thick warm oil,

Human wreckage on fertile soil.

I see the sun, it still shines bright.

As vultures over my carcass fight.

My crushed, chromed bike reflects the light.
Now I'm an Angel, and I'm alright.

Animal

A far

I write to you from a far country,

It has no pictures to give you,

It gives you not a thought to think.

I write to you from a lonely room,

Yet there are people here.

I write to you from a prison cell,

It is indeed, a far country.

Animal

Revenge

Fruupp in freedom, bars abounding,

Clock on concrete, ticking, surrounding.

Angel sprawls with spanner poised,

What masterpiece is about to arise.

Hot blood drips blackly upon the floor,

From a metal heart that beats no more.

All through the night he weaves his spell

On a hunk of metal he knows so well.

To well he recalls his chapters last stand

How his ol' lady died fighting; at his right hand,

He only feels revenge & hate,

For he will settle that outlaws fate.

The cold morning wind blows through his hair

As his metal beast vibrates with care

Faded colours upon his back, black smoke pours from his polished stack.

Out he rides, far into the west,

One last Brother, on a hopeless quest.

Animal

Brothers

You can feel it all around you, the oneness.

Apart, we are just different, yet each unique.

But together we ride as one, completely aware of all;

One mighty front to the dangers and the hassles;

Closer than blood, honor and righteousness between us;

Pride in belonging.

A right we defend with our lives, –

The Oneness – as Brothers.

John. N.M.C.

22

Queens Of The House

She sits in the kitchen
The queen of the house,
Who! My Tribsa Chop,
Who the fuck else!

Animal

Lost!

Tinkle, tinkle little part,

How I wonder were thou art.

I heard you hit the fucking ground

Then you disapeared, without a sound!

John

Skid Lid Blues

(Fiction)

Your helmets on my mantle

And brother so are you,

Your stuffed inside like sausage

With the consistancy of glue.

I found your hand just yesterday

And gave your thumb a clasp,

But you responded not at all

You didn't even laugh.

I've been looking for your peepers

To see if they show surprise,

And give them to your mother

(You said you had her eyes).

You used to be so talkative

You never shut your gap!

But now you cannot talk at all

Your mouth is held in by the strap.

I searched along the hedge row

The ditches and the trees,

So far I've found your ears and teeth

And your motorcycle keys.

I found all that I was looking for

Everything that once was you,

I still wont cease to call you Ralph

Even though your more like Stew.

Your all wedged in there pretty good

Though you sometimes overflow,

When a breeze comes through the window

And rocks the helmet to and fro.

But still I sleep more soundly now

Like a child, like a wail,

Because this helmet law I'm reading

Says your absolutely safe.

Animal

Freezer Heaven

(Fiction)

Babe your so cold tonight

As I hold you close in the freezers light,

Your lips are stilled in mockery

Of the girl I knew, so wild & free.

The soft covers I remember so well

Now hard & rough & cold as hell,

But I'm stuck on you & get my way

Coz you really don't have much to say.

And when I squeeze you in my arms

You freeze me with your evil charms,

Your cute, your cool, your cold as ice

But babe your still my paradise.

An if I live till I'm ninety—seven,

You'll still be here,..... in my freezer heaven.

Animal March 81

27

Goodbye!

Goodbye Easy Rider

You know I'll missy you for a while,

But the road is long.....

And my heart is strong,

I'll soon forget you babe.

(Uriah Heep)
For Easy rider,
Words taken from L.P. Sweet Freedom.

Norton Commando 850

I saw you in the pale moonlight,

A sparkled shimmer, soft, silver bright.

A wraith of fantasy & dream

Like early strawberries with Devon cream.

Your smooth curves both low & long,

In flight so smooth, a lark in song.

And yet beneath in deep dark sleep

A metal heart of thunderous beat,

Although now silenced is that roar

Forever awaiting for freedoms call.

In love she's warm, yet hard & cold,

In sunlight proud, like steeds of old.

She'll bitch & kick, then weave & soar

She'll answer to full all lifes foul score.

Animal (Summer 81)

If freedom is an illusion caused through caused through excessive consumption of alcohol, and reality is a pain in the arse. Who is to say that drink is evil!

Fresh Ass

Eat, sleep, fuck, schmuck,

Ooze booze, gaze, daze,

Smoke, choke, croak.

Roach, curve, speed exceed,

Screech, squeal, shattered steel!

Ripped, torn, blood,.....reborn!

Wrench, gaze, bruised, abraised,

Chrome dip, spray, quiet!

Eat, shit, sleep, creep.

Blood, oil, sweat, toil.....

Soft fox, furry box

Grass, ass, fucking gas,

Fly, sky, cry.

Rag rat, little brat,

Smell, stink, piss, howl.

Roaring, pounding, head, split!

Air, gass, fresh ass.

Eat, sleep, fuck, schmuck,

Ooze booze, gaze, daze,

Smoke, croak, choke.....

Animal (Summer 81)

Saddle Tramp

I've seen the sun & rode the rain,

Felt the highways hurt, & cried in pain.

I've seen the sky cry dirty tears,

For I've been there, for many years.

A little bit of everywhere, I remember here,

But as to where I'm goin', that ain't so clear.

I'm just a highway gypsy,

      a wandering vagabond.

All I own is with me,

      loving to hear the highways song.

I've been loved & hated,

Grown impatient, & I've waited.

Had my ups & had my downs,

I've heard the early morning sounds.....

Of things I felt I'd needed,

Of love as I was leaving.

Animal

Born Free

Born free, he rides through the years

Past bullets, babies, and ol' ladies tears.

He's of a proud kind with little to fear

And loves the road's song when done shifting gears.

He rides hard till his destination is met,

Harbouring memories he'll not soon forget.

The road is his home, as endless as time,

He's free from the hassles & has piece of mind.

Riding to live, & living to ride,

The wind's at his heels, & the stars are his guide.

Animal

Start You!

With gas tank full,
And battery charged,
Carefully set carbs,
And new plugs,
The points cleaned,
Wiring checked,
Contacts gauged,
Condenser replaced,
Float adjusted –
The bastard won't start!

The bastard started,
The ol' lady sighed,
Night was coming,
It was time to ride.

A single beam glow,
Against the asphalts sheen,
A token guiding light –
Into blackened night.

Animal

Goin' Home!

Its been a few years & a lot more beers,

So I get on my bike & ride,

To the old homestead where I first poked my head

And by rights where I should be tied.

I get there at last, but I just ride on past,

Knowing what I've become.

After ten thousand miles, and a lot less smiles,

I'm a biker son on the run.

(for my folks)

<u>Animal</u>

Saddle Tramp (2)

Riding nowhere,

Wind in your hair,

Bugs in your teeth,

Your beast underneath.

Thoughts in your head,

Respect for the dead,

Rock of all ages,

Escape from the cage's,

Born to be wild,

Destiny's child.

Roll out your mind,

Leave it behind,

Stay on the track,

Never look back,

Lighten your load,

Live on the road.

Animal

Jammin'

Jammin down the motorway,
Cruisin' about 75,
Weavin through the traffic,
Its great to be alive.

Guided by a beam of light,
Screamin' into turns,
Ridin' on a starlit night,
Listenin', to that engine chum.

Life on the road is hard but free,
A life thats cursed & damned,
I'm called trash and trouble –
But a Biker is what I am!

Animal

For Rose

Not long ago, or far away,

I met a chick who would ride all day.

She liked bikes, & weed to toke,

And while I was with her I never went broke.

Rose was good, and her body was fine,

And recently she's been on my mind.

Animal
(Spring 81)

Treasure Honey

Hey sweet lady, how are you?

Thought I'd drop in while pourin' through,

Been out followin' the ol' white line

An' thought of you from time to time.

You should have seen the forests in spring

The mountains smile & the birds all sing.

But when it comes down to you & me,

Your the finest thing I'll ever see.

The highway seems always to lead to your door,

Your good lovin' always makes me want for more.

Its always the same, so glad to see you,

Another face, another name, sure hate to leave you.

One may be blonde, another brown –

Seems I got one waitin', in most every town.

It might seem just a game I play,

But I love them all in my own special way.

Its good to know most places there'll be

Some pretty lady waitin' for me.

Animal

38

Goodbye Blues (Revised) Dianne

Whiteline fever made me leave her, but it was her choice
I told her I was goin' in a plain & simple voice.
I told her that I loved her, & I really was sincere,
But I also love the open road, & windsong in my ear.

I said that she could come along, & I hoped she would,
But I was splittin either way, & I'd be gone for good.
I didn't want to leave her – wasn't that at all –
But there was changes in the air, I heard the highway call.

I told her I was headin' out, & no, I'd not be back,

She was free to come with me, I'd wait for her to pack.

I told her I'd been listening to the wind that whispered by,

I told her I felt stifled & asked her not to cry.

I said I couldn't breath hemmed in, I didn't want a home,
Mine was the Creed of a Nomad, that needed space to roam,
I said I wanted to drift awhile, to wander far & wide,
I said I needed freedom, & that I had to ride.

I told her the time had come for me to drift away,
I told her once before it would, & now it was that day.
I said I'd been dreamin', of sights I'd never seen,
I said I had room for her, that she could share my dream.

P.T.O.

Yes she'd made me happy, no, she'd not done wrong,

Then I said I was sorry that she couldn't hear my song.

I said I knew I'd miss her, & I wished she couldn't cry,

Then I hugged her, & I kissed her, & bid her sweet goodbye.

(To Little Muff, for 6 good years)

Animal

Rolling Thunder

Rolling thunder,
Gleaming metal,
Slicing through the wind.

Soaring, roaring,
Cruising, gliding,
May it never end.

Ever riding,
Always moving,
Be forever free.

Bikes & bikers,
Chrome & leather,
Only way to be.

Animal

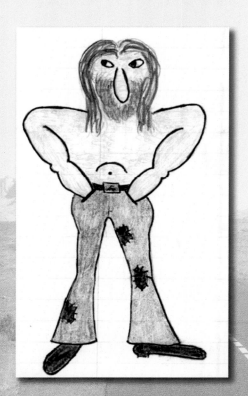

Brothers Of The Wind

I sit by the grave and listen,
To the rustle of the wind.
I hear dead brothers voices
Calling my name again.
I look up into the blue sky
With tears in my eye's,
Hopeing to see Heaven's Horsemen
Riding across the skies.
I think of guys & sisters
Brothers tried & true,
Their embraces of brotherhood,
And the good times we knew.

We rode together, brothers of the wind,
And someday, brothers, we'll ride again.

Animal

For   Chalky
      Geronimo
      Saint
      Sprocket
      Obelisk
      Zombie
      Easyrider
      Flash
      Little Starr
      Chiefy hee (A Boo in Move than name)
      (Hastings)
      ALL Bro's & Sister's of N.M.C.

Power Ride

Your sittin in your saddle
    feet up on the pegs,
Eight fifty cubic centimetres of power
    Are inbetween your legs.
You ride along the highway
    without a single care,
The straits they don't hassle you –
    you know they wouldn't dare.
Your ridin' with your brothers,
    your haired be blowin' free,
But you gotta wear fuckin' helmets
    with which you don't agree.
Your riding on your Norton
    The world can go get fucked.
And if any chicken climbs aboard,
    She knows she's gonna get plucked.

Animal

43

One step ahead of the Reapers blade,
Born to be different – A Renegade!

Animal

Pick-Up

Pretty baby, won't ya rap to me?

Pretty baby, won't ya ride with me?

Pretty baby, party please

Untill I know, whats behind that tease?

Pretty baby, won't ya toke with me?

Pretty baby, won't ya snort with me?

Pretty babe, you look so invitin',

We'll take my bike, she's fast as lightnin;

Pretty baby, I'm no dog,

Pretty baby, come ride my hog,

Pretty baby, lets split the fog,

Co's we'll ride an' ride till we're satisfied.

Animal

Tune Up

Every bikes in tune,

The sun is shinin',

Motorcycle women, wine,

And riding –

The weekends here again.

Animal

Sweet Hitch-Hiker

Soft, rich lustre,

Gentle waves flickering in the sun,

Her mane, a waterfall of highlights.

It caught my eye.

Her expression was light,

Exuberant,

A bright smile glistened a warm hello,

A natural blush made her cheeks shine,

A light heart shone all over a beautiful face

Adorned with flickering blue eyes.

I geared down.

She was walking.

Long, soft—but in shape legs carried her lightly

She turned slightly.

I hit my brakes.

Her breasts moved slightly –
The kind of movement.....
I like in the palm of my hand.

Her nipples poked
At her tight tank top.

My heart began to pound.

Her lips indicated gently that it wouldn't be the first time –
But it might be a helluva time,
The way her tight denim shorts undulated.
She was a beautiful sight,
Young 'n' tight.
        I rolled to a halt.....smiled.

My heart was workin' out
And my brow began to sweat:
I was in love,
And hadn't even met her yet!

Animal

48

Thats Life

There ain't no end to payin' dues,

Regardless of the road you choose.

Go one way, run out of gas,

Go another, loose your ass.

Stop a while, find a honey

Settle down, spend your money.

When its gone yer chick will sob,

And cross her legs till ya get a job.

Pack it in, hit the wind,

The law you learn calls livin' sin.

They can't stand it, don't ya know,

When your free to come & go.

Just because of who you are,

Runnin' wild and rangin' far,

It don't much matter what you do:

Sooner or later, jail for you.

Do your time and start again,

Where your goin' is where you've been.

Damn old worlds a merry-go-round –

All you can do is ride it down.

Animal

49

Progress (A Protest)

An eagle soared above the clouds,
As on a hill a lone wolf howled.
The sky was blue and sunny gold,
And down the highway thunder rolled.

There came a rider on the wind,
Like his olden pagan kin,
Who wandered lands of ages gone,
When men of freedom freely roamed.

The world was then a younger place,
With room to breath and elbow space.
Now, it seems, its shrunk a bit,
Till there's hardly room to shit!

In times gone by a man could run
From dawn till darkness took the sun,
And wander far and wide as free
As his own wild blood did choose to be.

But now the 'Nomads' world is bound
By walls and fences all around,
And in the name of legal right,
The law itself dims freedoms light.

P.T.O.

No more do gypsies rove at will,
And wolves no longer roam the hills;
These days the eagles seldom fly
Across the vastness of the sky.

They call it progress, all this change
That cages wolves & fences range,
And Eagles now are mighty rare;
Only a few still fly up there.

The land itself is locked uptight
By laws that say that black is white,
And up is down and sideways too,
And wrong is right & lies are true.

The very hills have been torn down
To put the earth on equal ground,
And men are taught to play the game,
To follow rules and not complain.

Pay your taxes, walk don't run;
And don't get busted having fun,
Be just like the other guy,
And watch T.V. untill you die.

Animal
Summer 81

No Way Out (A TRUE TALE?)

I was layin' and playin'
With a foxy lady
An' the trash I was sayin'
Was drivin' her crazy.
She said "'Animal' you do me right –
Ain't been loved good for many a night"
I said "Yeah baby your outa sight –
Just make ol' Animal feel allright."
Then the door burst open,
There stood a guy with a 60 inch chest.
I was a wishin' & a hopin'
He had the wrong address.
No way out – he was blockin' the door,
No way out – I was on the ninth floor.
I started coppin' a plea –
Said there must be some mistake.
But then he said to me,
"Your neck I'm gonna break."
The fox was yellin' for the pigs
Actin' like she was hurt,
Yellin' and pointin' at me,
Sayin' I was a Rapein' pervert.
The big guy started shakin'
An' I saw my chance,

P.T.O.

I took off like a dog on heat
An' left my pants rapped round his feet.

Animal
July 81

52

One for The Road

From break of dawn till day is gone
And moonlight lights the sky,
Somewhere out there on the road
A scooter tramp passes by.

He's here today, then gone away,
A jammin' in the wind.
He might return, or maybe not,
Dependin' on his whim.

He's got his bike & a bag of stuff
That lashes on the rear,
He owns what's in his pockets –
Thats all his worldly gear.

He lives a life that suits him well
And hopes yours fits the same,
But if it don't, don't cry to him,
Co's he sure ain't to blame.

The only one he's runnin's his,
And his is on the run,
For God made roads to travel on,
And he's a faithfull son.

Animal

Brothers (2)

Share the good times and the bad,

Share the love and the hate,

Share the work and the rewards,

Share the fifth and the brew,

Share the parts and the chrome,

Share the women and the drugs,

He's your brother,

Always at your back,

Hangin' in there,

Takin' up the slack.

Animal

In The Wind

He eats when he's hungary & scowls when he's mean,
He's kinda good lookin' but he ain't awfull clean.
His eye's are wind squinted from years on the road,
And there's places he's wanted for wild oats he's rowed.

His name doesn't matter, coz whats a name?
He limps just a tad, but he sure ain't lame.
He's geared like a mule, & wrong more than right,
He's gooder than gold, & pure hell in a fight.

His knuckles are bony, his hairs gettin' thin,
But he's in good shape, for the shape that he's in,
His heart is as strong as a cylinder wall,
And if a bro needs him he'll ride to the call.

He works when he has to equits when he can,
He dreams his own dreams, & stays his own man,
The highway's his heaven, his creed's brotherhood,
And he'd gladly ride forever, if only he could.

The routes that he's travelled and mapped in his head,
And so are the bar's & backrooms, & beds,
The things that he's done, & the places he's been,
Have marked him a brave man, & not scared of sin.

He drinks when he's thirsty, & whoops when he's high
Scratches his itches, & graps for the sky.
He cares not a damn for most of the world,
Just friends, & wind, & those fiery—eyed girls.

He'll go where he's headin' & make his own way,
The same as he's done since his growin' up day.
He'll take no advice, & he won't wash his feet,
He never backs up or admits that he's beat.

He'll wrench ti'll he's ragged to build a top mill,
And stand by a brother ti'll hell takes a chill.
He's raunchy & righteous, a hundred-proof man,
And he'll ride forever, if anyone can.

Animal

Freedom Breeze ①

Ridin' free,

Wind in my hair,

Two wheels only,

And not one care.

Out past the traffic,

I let out a cry,

The sun looks down

As I roar by.

Blowin' the hassles

Out of my mind,

Once on the road

Leavin' city behind.

Up in the mountains,

The curves & the hills,

Just me and my bike,

Gettin' our thrills.

Animal

Freedom Breeze (2)

Feel the wind blow.
Even the skie's know
The free soul you are.
Shuckin' & jivin';
Some real hard ridin'!
Got to follow your lucky star.
Got a sweet lovin' mama
Who makes ya just wanna
Look into her sparklin' eye's.
A drink from the bottle,
A twist of the throttle,
And your ready to fly.
Head full of good dreams
As the highway screams
Past with hurricane power.
Yeah! a real prancer,
A white line dancer,
At a hundred ten miles an hour.
He's his own keeper,
Doesn't fear the reaper,
Lets his spirit ride free.
Love's to keep driftin,
Hear gears a—shiftin;
To keep in perfect harmony.

Animal

Down Time

Well, old friend, its been a while

Since we rode the highways

And partied in style.

I know you can't forget

How those times used to be,

On the hot summer nights

When we were both free.

Your tank is probably dusty

And your chrome could use a shine,

But don't start getting worried –

You will always be mine.

So you just take it easy,

Me,! I'll do the same.

Ol' friend, I can hardly wait

Till I'm back on your frame.

Animal (78)

Fuck It!

My expensive stash was half baking powder,

A bro broke my new cast iron disc,

The fridge ain't got no cold beers,

And the ol' lady won't screw on the rag.

The unemployment ain't come yet,

And my hearts still giving me shit,

The power was turned off yesterday,

I ain't gettin' outa bed – fuck it.

Animal

Death

We mock death –

Laugh in its face,

Wear his symbols

To show we ain't afraid.

Citizens run from him,

They pray he won't come.

But he packs on our shoulders

Each time we cross town.

He's on our backs

In front of our wheels,

He's reachin out

Snappin' at our heels.

But by god we'll ride harder

Rougher roads we'll seek,

P.T.O.

The more danger the better –

Death won't ever call us weak.

Animal

Getting Hitched

A gallon of cider & some take away chow,
Mebbe some smoke, & me and thou.
A breeze kissed putt on a sunny day,
To a shady spot where we can play.

We'll smoke and joke and carry on;
I'll tell you poems & sing you songs.
We'll take a stroll, then lay us down.
And check out Heaven from the ground.

The clouds will float across the sky,
In picture shapes for you and I.
Our bodies will meet, our lips will kiss,
And hours we'll spend in perfect bliss.

We'll ride some more, then stop again,
To hear the music in the wind.
We'll talk awhile, of lovers things,
And of the sadness parting brings.

At the end of day I'll take you home,
Then say goodbye, and I'll be gone.
Tomorrow you will be a bride,
But today your mine, for one last ride.

(For Shaz)

Animal

62

Windsong

Listen closely,

The wind is telling

Those who care

About where its been,

The lives, it's shared,

The freedom its seen.

Cruising, roaring

Laughing & soaring...

You've asked me

Where I'd rather be,

And my answer...

In the wind.

Animal

Easyrider

The wind sings through my hair

In sunshine, snow, & rain,

Through the never-ending city streets

Freeways, farm tracks, & big three lanes.

I really like this feeling of being completely free,

And no matter where I end up,

It's where I want to be.

I've got a headfull of dreams

Just like any other man.

I ride them down, one by one,

And hold them in my hand.

So let my boot heels dance

Across an endless sky.

And let me ride my iron horse

Untill the day I die.

Animal

Forgotten Army Or

(Where has all our freedom gone!)

With burning love you live a life

With foxy women, hassle & strife,

With shiny bikes & crazy chicks

We all live free, in Her Majesties nicks.

For living wild & riding free

We all get busted, how can that be?

This is a free country the politicians say

Then pass another law to keep things their way.

Our fathers fought in two world wars

Now yesterdays heroes have to beg at our doors,

The forgotten army who fought to keep us free

Now stand at street corners with a "spare a copper plea."

Its a country suppressed, what did they fight to save?

Lifes just a pain in the arse; on the way to the grave!

Animal

Reason

New faces, a new town, but its just the same,

Life still goes on in the same old grain.

The same old problems, you know the score

Another pint, another joint there must be more!

Find a new chick, she'll just turn round & say

The same as the last at the end of the day,

You've done it all, at only twenty—five

So you need a new reason to continue, to survive.

Animal

Stoned Again ①

They opened their mouths.....

and tanks came forth, belching flames,

I wanted cars with furry doors

to escape the violence next door.

You see, a javelin came through the wall.

They offered chocolate biscuits

For £30 a day, they were slimy & comfortable

Then.....the tanks got me.

Animal

Stoned Again (2) & Beyond

They opened their mouths
And tanks came forth belching flames,
I wanted cars with furry doors
To escape the violence next door.
You see..... javelins were coming through the walls.
I hired a chocolate biscuit
For £30 a day,
It was slimy and comfortable.
The fire had melted me, unknowingly,
I flowed into the hall,
The floor.....wasn't there.....air.....
I floated.....raising.....colours.....
More colours.....rushing wind.....sound.....
Is this.....can it be.....trancendance!
Sparks glow.....sparkle.....getting brighter.
I arrive, I know, I am.....vast expances
And knowledge crowd my.....my mind?
Yes! and no, for I am, everything is.....part of me.
I have met god, for I am god!
The memories aeons old piece together.
The crash, I remember the crash,
Systems failing, power, must generate more power.....
And finally the core failure.
We plunge through a dense atmosphere.

P.T.O.

Carbon life forms abound
And we disperse, absorbed.
Legends are written about us,
Crewd drawings adorn cave walls.
In time, a few of us through our hosts
Make ourselves known,
Attempt to teach those we do not occupy.
We are killed, crucified.
Are we, the all knowing, all powerfull, trapped?
Trapped in the very carbon based life forms
That offer our only chance of continuity.
Years upon years of hints, searching, always searching.
The flames recede.....
Cars I want cars with furry doors,
No.....wait, the violence is inside me.
I feel loss, huge, empty, loss.....
There is something.....something
I must remember,
But its gone.
A fix.....must get.....remember.....

Animal

Foot Note:-

An astronaut, from where we know not, once played GOD to us, Now do we not also play GOD to those with less knowledge & power than ourselves.

Animal

My Dog

Well you can nag, nag, nag,

You dirty old hag,

You slithering slimy slut!

May maggots lie between your thighs

And fester in your butt.

I'd rather drink dead mens puke

Than suck your slimy clit

And everytime I see your face

I think of vulture shit.

Animal

Desire

Reality is a dirty word.

Celibacy is trite.

I desire to touch her,

And tell her so one night.

She makes her world seem logical,

Requiring me to reckon.

She tries to content me,

But I feel my freedom beckon.

I can't hold still to even try,

Because I'm only passing by.

Suburban life ain't worth a dime.

Another place, another time.

(For Toni.)

Animal

71

Lock down (2 Poems from the Pen)

I want to be on the road again,

If only for a while.

I want to be in the wind again,

If only for a mile.

I want to be free to enjoy my life,

For nothing else can provide

The satisfaction that I get

When I go for a ride.

Animal
(Feb 82)

Detour
(For Crazy Kate)

I took a detour somewhere;

I almost lost my way,

And if it had not been for you

I might have had to stay.

A Zombie, doped and serialised

A blend with prison bricks,

A stagnant 12 hour routine,

No life, no love, no kicks.

Theres freedom now in all I do

And my heart is not a liar,

In gratitude I live each day

As wild as mountain fire.

Animal
(Feb 82)

Highway Queen

I had an idea of what was in store,

So I waited untill you had grew up some more.

At last you attained the age of sixteen,

I said you could be my new highway queen.

You gave your consent and your virginal heart,

We rode to the place where our new life could start.

You kissed me so sweetly, I turned off the light,

You whispered you loved me & said I was right.

To be there close to you, to go all the way,

We had waited years for this special day.

The pleasure & passion you would soon reveal,

Caused you to shiver & daintily squeal.

The thought of you'r body put stars in my head,

Then I reached out to touch you, and fell off the bed.

(Little Muff 74)

Animal

74

The Walls

The walls close in on me.

I feel my freedom beckon

Calling me like a lost lover,

For the pain is the same.

Animal

Big Brother

The world needs a hero & free livin' men

Who don't require money to save us from sin,

We have a big brother who makes all the rules

But he's not happy & calls us all fools.

He's abolished freedom & our fate seems worse

Endangered all strangers born with the same curse,

He readily damns & lables profane

The lifestyle we cherish to keep us all sane.

Statistics are rampant, truths lost its core

His power games pimp the minority whore,

Meanwhile, the doctrines he's based on bleed

And apathy keeps him from all but his greed.

The world needs a 'biker' to give it a ride,

And maybe to show it why we have such pride.

Animal
(Feb 82)

Fate

You have me now chained
To these four little walls,
But I will rise again!
Six months you said,
Then six again.
But who really controls my lifes chain,
For I will raise again!
To pull your hearts out!
Now, whos really insane?
Me or you?
Shall I open the door, or wait?
Coz you bastards haven't the bottle
To meet me at the gate!

Animal
Ex. N.M.C.
(Aug 81 June 82)
Adapted from a poem by FREEWHEELIN' FRANK,
FRISCO CHAPTER, HELL'S ANGELS.
CALIFORNIA. U.S.A.

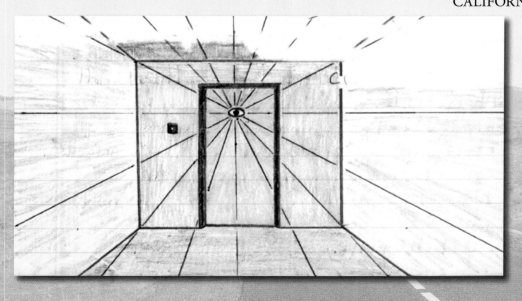

A Poem

There are thieves,

But there are two sides

In the night,

Both of them can walk.

Only one

Will have a light shining.

For guilt

Has been handed

Only from one palm.

The thief of righteousness

Shall never have to feel guilt,

For his love is with his feelings

And in turn he can always look up

With never even a thought of looking back.

I, A Hell's Angel, feel I have over me

Guardian Angels.

Even we have lost Angels from this Earth

Which is Hell.

by FREEWHEELIN' FRANK,
FRISCO CHAPTER, HELL'S ANGELS.
CALIFORNIA, U.S.A.

Memories

Cruising down the highway
Jamming about ninety–five
Leaving the dirty city
It's great to be alive.

Heading for the country
A place thats wild and free
Leaving behind the hassles
Just my bike, ol' lady and me.

Lazing in the meadows
Splashing in the stream
With good old camp fire cooking
And a bottle of Jim Beam.

Camping under the moonlight
With stars out over–head,
I hold her close to me.....
She whispers, "time for bed."

Animal
(Written in Leicester Prison, March 82.)
(for Ariel, summer of 81)

This is what the proof of 'Goodbye Blues' came out like, I enter it coz its about, and for, a very special person.

I said that I was leaving

In a plain and simple voice,

I said I didn't want to

But I simply had no choice.

I didn't want to hurt her

I said she could come with me

There are still too many places

I have yet to see.

I said I'd hold a little while

And wait for her to pack,

She cried and in a broken voice

Asked when I'd be back.

She asked if she'd done wrong

I replied, "no, not at all,"

But the road was in my blood

I had heard the highways call.

I told her that I loved her

And asked her not to cry,

Then I kissed her and caressed her

And bid her sweet goodbye.

(for Little Muff.)

Animal

The Ballad of Billy Joe.

(Fiction)

Billy Joe was a 'biker'
Tall, scarred, and mean,
He rode a black Tribsa chop
Some called his killing machine.
With his long black hair and matted beard
Billy was fast, and his bro's said weird.
Hells highways he rode
And rougher roads he sought,
And so the tale goes
Thats how he got caught.
Well the Devil one night he stopped Billy Joe
He said, "Your a flash bastard and I want you to know,
But you live your life hard and don't give a damn
So a solid gold hog I'm giving you man.
But when your time comes I'll be looking for you
Coz your sole is now mine and thats my due."
Now Billy don't scare and he flashed a scowl
And the demons in Hell you could here them howl,
He said, "Get this Devil, that bikes my right!"
So he rode it away that very same night.
Now one of Billy's bro's was a guy called 'Cam'
And lust for that bike made him hatch a plan,
He was mean and fast
And pure hell in a fight
But that solid gold hog
Twisted his gut uptight.
A cross a lane at neck height can secured a wire
Hopeing Billy would hit it and then retire,
Toteting hundred plus ten and spiting fire
Billy Joe lost his head on Cam's tight wire.
His blood dripping blackly on fertile soil

Billy just laughed, and Cam's blood did boil.
The flames of Hell devoured Cam that night
And Billy checked his head to see if it was alright.
He turned to his bro's and said there 'n' then
"If any of you mother fuckers try that again,
I'll string you all up from the highest tree".
The Devil did laugh and his host danced with glee.
Yeah Billy still rides that solid gold bike
And the Devils on his tail most every night,
Once a motorcycle cop tried to ride him down
But the ground opened up, he was lost without a sound.
So if late one night you hear a roar
Just hide up quiet and bolt the door,
Coz sure as Hell and that ain't no joke
It'll be Billy Joe belching flames and smoke.
With moonbeams to guide him
And stars in his eyes,
Billy Joe caged the Devil
And his host are his spies.

Animal

82

Limbo

I sit in this small cell and erupt,
The frustration crowd and rip
At my emotions, yet I am caged.
The walls close in on me.
The urge to break out
To be free.....
Builds up inside me to a violent pitch.
I bruise my knuckles on the walls
The warm red blood flowing
Out of my ripped flesh torments me.
I put my first through the window
Feeling no pain as the glass shatters.
The walls still close in.
I feel freedom beckon
Calling me like a lost lover,
For the pain is the same.
The pressure mounts
And I become afraid of insanity,
The restlessness stirs inside me.
My whole being is trapped in a vacuum
A limbo suspended in space and time,
And I have not even the stars
To keep me company.

Animal
April 82

83

Eternal Night

A silver shaft illuminates the door.
I lie in my bunk, with memories of you.
I see your golden locks sparkle in summer sun,
Your knowing smile, and the tease in your eyes

It is December in my heart.

We touch, I feel your soft carress.
The warmth of your body against mine,
And your urgency.

The chill and damp invade my soul.

Your lips seek mine,
I drown in your kiss,
Our bodies arch in, (for me,) long forgotten passion.

The cardboard sheets rasp against my skin.

The moonbeams of eternal light
Play witness to my thoughts of you,
And share my memories.

(for Ariel)

Animal

84

Amra, dragon slayer

(I)

The dragons spread, from the dim, far west
And only fools stood against their quest,
Bedecked with tentacle and flame
Zilgar in search of Amra came.

Flying high in glory, bronze and gold
Diving entwined to seize and hold,
A strand of silver in the sky
From which all cowards quickly fly.

Sawdust, gold dust twist in heated air
Waste dust, wind rushed strips you bare,
Wheel and turn, or bleed and burn
Soaring dragons cause mortals to squirm.

While on halls both dark and deep
The God of Light awakes from sleep,
Amra roared and legions came
Formed from warriors laid aeons slain.

A fleck of red, in a cold night sky
A drop of blood to guide them by,
Turn away and run, dragons be gone
For Amra beckons his warriors on.

Gone away or gone ahead
Where have all the dragons fled,
Flying high on silvery wing,
Amra laughs, his warriors sing.

The honour of the dragon pack heeds

In thought and favour, word and deed,
Amras won, the dragons are lost
Zilgars flame is nought but frost.

But wait and watch, for wise men learn
Something new in every turn,
Zilgars old, but his blood is blue
And fiery hearts still burn true.

A finger points at an eye blood red
Alert the warriors to a silver thread.
Seas boil up and mountains fall
For now Amra hears Zilgars roar.

(II)

By the Golden Egg of Zilgar
Rise up my kin, wise and true
There a flight of bronze & brown wings
Here a flight of green & blue.

Birth Of Zilgar

Hell spawned riders, strong and daring
Dragon—loving, born as hatched,
A flight of hundreds soaring skywards
Man and Dragon fully matched.

The land is bared as all men vanish
The soil scorched barren, all hope banished
Free the flame and sear the grass
Untill the armies of Amra pass.

The blackest night must end in dawn
And sun dispel all warriors fear,
For when souls break in helpless pain
Amra thunders forth to revenge the slain.

Cold steel hisses, death—bearing
Dragons dieing in flight unguided
Amra roars, brave warriors swearing
For now the battle is twice decided

No—more will silvery threads up high
Spread terror through the Eastern sky,
The God of Light has fought again
And now the Dragons are truly slain.

Animal

Fallen Angel

When I was a fighting man
The battle drums they'd beat,
And people scattered gold dust
Before my horse's feet.

When I became a leader
The people barred my track,
With poison in my wine cup
And daggers in my back.

For my road runs out in thistle
And my dreams have turned to dust,
Now my steeds fade and falter
To the raven-wings of rust.

Animal
Ex; N.M.C.

The Run

We rode on the wind with the stars in our hair,

Like Death fell our shadow on villages and towns;

And the fools and their followers cry out in despair

For the hoofs of our stallions have trampled their crowns.

Animal

Revenge (2)

Iron winds and rain and flame,
And a Nomad shaking with giant mirth;
Over the corpse – strewn blackened earth
Death, stalking naked came.

Like a storm cloud, shattering ships,
Yet the Rider seated high,
Paled at the smile on a dead Outlaws lips
As his silver horse thundered by.

Animal

- <u>Kipling</u> -

What's yon, that follows at my side? —

The foe that ye must fight, my lord, —

That hirples swift as I can ride? —

The shadow of the night, my lord?

- Poe -

The searing glory which hath shone

Amid the jewels of my throne,

Halo of Hell! and with a pain

Not Hell shall make me fear again?

From; Tamerlane.

Citizen

Take stock;

Now that there are so many billions of you

Bleeding through your opened veins,

Into the bathtub, or into the sea

The cost you pay for imagining your free.

Ideas;

They raised you literate and educated

Equipped to exercise iniative,

But now our technological society

Insists you behave as a statistic.

Products;

It's not by any means improbable

You possess advanced skills and crafts,

But theres a tape in your chemical machine

To control the way you graft.

Reproduction;

Apply to the Citizen Processing Board

Give them a sample of your genotype,

But he prepared to here its disallowed

Cause they don't like your particular hype.

Death;

'Here lies the beloved.....of Mary

Mother of Jim and Jane',

But they closed the cemetery at Round Oak

And built a chimney, belching smoke.

Accomplishment;

Here is your monument, and it stands high

The cars you wore out, the clothes you tore,

The cans you emptied, the furniture you broke

And all the shit, on which your children now choke.

Animal

Mr & Mrs Everybody

Like the dictator 'God' in the valley of bones

They 'state' made some people and it called them Jones.

They were not alive and they were not dead

But the State said they were the way ahead.

It was unremarkable and not quite new

'Coz the state made them look like me and you.

Living their lives in a kind of trance

They put them in Mexico and put them in France.

Yeah; Mr & Mrs Jones, thats the right name

And a gadget in their heads make them act the same.

You can't visit all the places of intrest

Like a flight to the moon or Mount Everest.

You stay at home in a comfortable chair

And rely on Mr & Mrs Jones, coz their everywhere.

Doing all the things you would like to do

Coz a gadget in their heads makes them act like you.

When Mr & Mrs Jones crack a joke

It's laughed at by all right thinking folk.

When Mr & Mrs Jones adopt a pose

It's the with-it view as everyone knows.

It may be a rumour or it may be true

The gadget in your head says the jokes on you.

The World Wide Bureaucratic Service

Dont do this without any purpose,

They know exactly what they would like

A thousand million people all thinking alike.

Whatever your country or whatever your name

A gadget in your head makes you think the same.

Animal

Meeting At Night, Revisited

(For, Sweetheof)

The gray sea caresses the long black land

And the yellow half moon reflects large & low

On the gentle little waves that leap

In fiery ringlets from the deep.   (Browning)

I reach the cove with thunderous roar

And wait upon the golden sands

Wishing only to hear your call

And feel your body beneath my hands.

A gentle sigh upon the breeze

You soft football cries out to me,

And along the warm sea–scented beach

Our bodies for each other reach.

I tell you tales of dareing deeds,

You satisfy my earthly needs

Our hearts as one together beat

Whilst waves caress our bodies in heat

And when at dawn you softly sigh

'It's time for lovers to say goodbye'

You'll go your way with a tear,

And I'll go mine, for another year.

Animal

Reflection on Revenge

World all over, beautifull as the sky,

Beautifull that war and all its carnage

Must in time be forever lost,

And the hands of the sisters Death and Night

Will never wash again this fraught isle;

For an Outlaw is dead.

A man, once free as myself is dead,

I look where he lies white-faced and still

Coldly embraced in his earthen coffin,

And in exchange a spirit is freed.

Honour and righteousness has been fulfilled

Pursued to its savage end.

I, a Nomad and avenging Angel

Pay homage.....

To the white face in an earthen coffin.

Animal

And but for a twist of fate.....

there would lie I.

Changes

I have been young & now am not too old
For I have seen the righteous taken,
Their health, honour and quality weaken
We are now not what we formerly where.

I have seen a green country disgraced
Rode with guns & in peace through its towns,
Hid with the fox & run with the hounds
And law itself knows no bounds.

Mames

Two Views of The Same Stretch Of Canal

First Impression

A clot of oil, discarded tyre

The ugly twist of broken wire,

The plastic bag and tin of coke

On which nature will surely choke.

An old newspaper a bag of crisps

The chemical spillage trails and wisps,

Broken spars and rotting wood,

The bloated corpse of the misunderstood.

I walked beside the canal today,

I wished I had gone another way.

Second Impression.

Even the air is fresh, green, unsullied,

Time past and future merge

And the present, lasts forever.

Stark forbidden buildings,

The scars of industry

Ripple upon the surface of

Dark forgotten waterways.

Rushs throng the deserted banks

Clogging, hideing the narrow outlets

That once disgorged industries filth

Into these living waters.

Man; the betrayer of natures trust, has left,

But his hurt remains.

Where humans sweated

And horses labored to draw leaden loads

Plant and animal now weave their destiny,

A brown/black bird flecked with white

Jealously guards her fledgling chicks,

A swan glides majestically past,

The monarch of its domain.

Minuite insects dive, twist and soar

Along its quiet surface,

And below these still waters, who knows,

Nature has once again reclaimed her own.

Mames.
May/June 82

103

Watch Me!

Our minds are full of little boxs,

They tell us how to spend our money,

Tell us where to go on holiday.

What clothes to wear,

What to eat.

Fill our lives with blood and violence

And sex.

See tragedy unfold in your front room,

Watch me, I'll dispel your evenings gloom.

Brainwash your children.

Insult your intelligence.

Show you pleasures you can't afford,

Me, I'm your TV, you call me Lord.

Mames
June 82.

Why?

I are a Nomad, shall go always a little further.

It may be beyond the last blue mountain topped with snow,

Or across that angry or this sparkling sea.

Because somewhere, high on a throne, or deep in a cave,

There lives a prophet who can understand.....

Why men are born.

Mames

Venture

My mighty craft is winged in gold
A dragon of night—dark sky,
Swiftborn, dreambound and rudderless
Her master & crew are 1.

I've sailed a hundred restless tides
Where no seamans ever been,
And only my goldwinged craft and I
Know the marvels we have seen.

Animal

Denise

For the good of the life and the love in your heart,

For the good of the light in your eyes,

For the good of the welcome and warmth in your smile,

For the thrill of the chase on a moonlit night,

For the pleasure of holding your body so tight.

For the love of your children and a share of their dreams,

For the years that we've spent apart,

And for the hope of things yet to come

That still lies deep in my heart.

Animal

Runnin'

It's time to move on, see the pieces don't fit

One more lousy fix, yeh another lousy hit

And all I own is hangin' in my jeans

I'm gettin' so tired of the same old scenes.

My hot bike throbbin', scorchin' for the curves

Killer on the road ridin' on my nerves

I turn up my collar like a vampire bat

I've raced with the devil & the cold wind spat.

Runnin' like the crime of a switch blade knife

It seems I've been hunter or hunted all my life

Watchin' the shadows coz its one of my ways

The chasin' sun sinks & the daylight fades.

Animal

Soul Sister

Mango grove moon in the middle of June

Theres a high flyin' sister on my knee,

She don't want no favour

She's only here to savor

What I'm gonna give her for free.

I take a trip with the zip, straight from her hip

She's a switch bitch with no hitch

Flicks her hair back kinda kitsch

Soul suckin' temptress, she takes me down,

Love child of the night out on the town.

She said turn up the amps, turn down the lamps

She's just as wild as she may seem,

She grabbed my heart like a stone

Thrust me in her velvet zone,

Aint that just the cream on the dream.

Animal

Reflections

Hanging around in public rooms,
Waiting rooms,
Yeah! they really give me the glooms.
Do you know a better way to get free pay!

Spendin' my life on the motorway,
Hittin the white line.....
I've worn my types pretty thin that way.
My jeans too I guess.

Muddy waters washed my soul,
I've lain in the gutters & fried in the fire
Squandered my existence on lifes high wire.
I'd do it again.

Howd' you recognise the highs
Unless you've been down the drains,
And how do you recognise true love
Untill you've seen her in pain.....
And because of the situation, walked away.

(Thinking of you D.)

Animal
(Aug 82)

City

And now while the city dreamers sleep

I walk the dark road to the river,

The city sings the saddest song you'll ever hear.

The streets are empty now,

The night died long ago.

City, city

Is there anybody there?

(Leicester)

<u>Animal</u>
(82)

Dead End Street

Out on the street, dead on my feet

At the mercy of the stone cold night,

Its hard to compete, in a dead end street

With frustrations in your line of sight.

I followed a sign that pointed the way

And found myself right back at the start,

I like to feel good, I've tried feeling sad,

But I can't stand a broken heart.

A grey cloud they say hides a surprise

But it rained until I lost my belief,

So just close your eyes & I'll show you the way

That leads out of your dead end street.

(for Denise)

Animal
(Sept 82)

A Waiting

(For Denise)

I have often told you stories
About the way,
I lived the life of a nomad
Waiting for the day.
When I'd take your hand
And sing you songs,
Then maybe you would say.....
'Come lay with me and love me'
And I would surely stay.

Many years I've been a traveller
I looked for something new,
In days of old
When nights were cold
I wandered without you.
In those days I thought my eyes
Had seen you standing near,
But sight is so confusing
When it shows that your not here.

Theres something in the saying
That a woman needs a little more time,
But I've been so long awaiting
Please won't you give me some sign.

Animal
82

113

Farewell

The tears I feel today
I'll wait to shed tomorrow
Though I'll not sleep this night
Nor find ease from sorrow.
My eyes must keep their sight
I dare not be tear—blinded,
I must be free to talk
Not choked with grief, clear—minded.
My face cannot betray
This anguish that I know,
Yes, I'll keep my tears till later;
But my grief will never go.

(For Little Starr)

Animal

Why

You know who I am, you know what I do

I've travelled the country just looking for you,

I'm a love machine, my gazes are hot

You know what I mean, the waiting must stop

The lights are like beads, laced to the sky

I wait for your needs, I wait for your eye,

The sunset and I are dim for a while

But we'll burn again babe, much more in our style.

The sheep who walk by, they smile I know why

Stray meat on the prowl, out lookin' for highs

I've checked out the bars, I've checked out the beer,

I've checked out this town babe,

Oh why aren't you here.

Animal

Painted Lady

Serene & slow they chug along

The painted ladies of my song,

With hearts of Ash and Elm or Oak

Or other timber of lesser note.

Upon river canal or creek

You'll see them almost every week,

Gracefull Nomad's of the waterways

Thats how I'd like to end my days.

A home afloat to travel where

My heart would voyage in weather fair.

Mames

Last Word

They may take me away

And lock me uptight,

Deprive me of day

And rob me of night.

The Imperial Wizard

Sits on his high throne,

Defiles my freedom

And breaks up my home.

But the 'Old God's' are with me

And rights on my side,

For the freedom to live

And the freedom to ride.

This I feel deep inside me

And that ain't no lie,

But what they'll never take away

Is our freedom to die.

Animal

Enemies can often strengthen you, while allies weaken you......

It has occurred to me our ancestors were survivors, and survival itself involves savage decisions, a brutality civilization works hard to suppress. The price we pay for that suppression could be our own extinction.

The problem of leadership is: - who will play God? For was he not the ultimate dictator.

Most civilization is based on cowardice. You water down the standards which would lead to bravery. You restrain the will. You regulate appetites and fence in the horizons. You make a law for every movement. You deny the existence of free will, even the children are taught to follow rules and not complain.

This universe presents only changing relationships, which are sometimes seen as laws by such short-lived chemical awarenesses as ourselves. We are fleetingly aware of temporary conditions which confine (at present) our activities. So if we must lable the absolute why not use its proper name; temporary.

I was once asked if my lifestyle was that of a responsible person, my answer is; responsibility is able to respond, able to answer for the way I choose to live my life. Of course the only person I have to answer to is myself. As you must answer to yourselves. If I can satisfy myself that what I choose to do is right, then yes, my lifestyle is responsible.

Do-not think that this is an easy thing, for if you lie, or cheat yourself to avoid responsibility do not expect trust or respect from others.

Animal,

Ex, Nomads M.C.

We are what we are because each of us chose to be so.

This book is based on fact, a little fantasy, and entirely on the belief that we exist not to impress the world, but to live our lives in a way that will make us happy.

The club to which I are proud to have belonged is now operating under a different name, with different values, which many of my Brothers who left at the same time as I did feel we can no longer offer our support. For those brothers and the few 'Nomads' who changed colours to try and guide the new club with the benefit of their experience this book is ultimatly dedicated.

Animal
Ex, N.M.C.

Freedom.....the first gift given to man, and man was the first to take it away.

Mames

Printed in the United States
By Bookmasters